EXPLORING THE PAST

The MIDDLE AGES

CATHERINE OAKES

ILLUSTRATED BY STEPHEN BIESTY

GULLIVER BOOKS
HARCOURT BRACE JOVANOVICH, PUBLISHERS
San Diego   New York   London

HBJ

First published 1989 by The Hamlyn Publishing Group Limited
Copyright © 1989 by The Hamlyn Publishing Group Limited

Library of Congress Cataloging-in-Publication Data
Oakes, Catherine.
Exploring the past : the Middle Ages / by Catherine Oakes :
illustrated by Stephen Biesty.
p.   cm.
"Gulliver books."
Includes index.
Summary: An overview of life in the Middle Ages,
describing the arts and learning, religion, trading
and exploration, nobility, and life in the country,
in the towns, and in the wider world.
ISBN 0-15-200451-3
1. Civilization, Medieval—Juvenile literature.
[1. Civilization, Medieval. 2. Middle Ages.] I. Biesty, Stephen,
ill. II. Title.
CB351.023 1989
909.07—dc19   88-30075

Produced by Mandarin Offset
Printed and bound in Hong Kong

First U.S. edition 1989
A B C D E

CONTENTS

Introduction 4

The Arts and Learning 6
A Child's Education 8
Universities 9
What People Thought 10
Making a Book 12
Artists and Paintings 13

Religion 14
Monks and Nuns 16
The Luxurious Houses of God 18
Saints and Pilgrims 20
Crusaders and Heretics 22

Life of the Nobility 24
Kings, Lords, and Barons 26
Knights and Tournaments 28
Feasts 30
Entertainment 32

Life in the Country 34

The Lord and His Manor 36
Peasants at Work 38
Peasants at Home 40

Life in the Towns 42
Buying and Selling 44
The Guilds 46
Entertainment 47
Family Life 48
What People Wore 49
Health and Healing 50

The Wider World 52
Navigators and Explorers 54
Trading with Distant Lands 56
New Discoveries and Inventions 58

Piecing the Clues Together 60

Time Chart 62

Index 64

INTRODUCTION

This book is about the "Middle Ages," or the "Medieval World," as it is often called. Both names mean the period or "the time in-between" the colorful days of the Roman Empire and the important years of the Renaissance. Long ago, people thought the Middle Ages was an insignificant time when nothing important happened. Today we know better. In fact, the Middle Ages lasted for almost 1,000 years during which time many exciting things happened.

We have to hunt hard for "evidence" to tell us what it was like to live even 100 years ago — let alone in the Middle Ages, over 1,000 years ago! Try making a note of everything at home that depends upon electricity, for example. Of course, if you look, there are important pieces of evidence and many clues you can find. Historians study old documents, records, and books to find out about the Middle Ages. Visiting old buildings, going to museums, or looking at old paintings can help you to

JANUARY

APRIL

FEBRUARY

MAY

MARCH

JUNE

imagine what it was like in the Middle Ages. But most important of all, we need to use our imaginations to rediscover the past and to understand just what it was like to live then.

To start, try to picture a world with far fewer people, where families lived together much longer and didn't move away from their home town; where most ordinary people worked as farmers; where everything happened slowly. Imagine what it would be like to live without electric lights, water from the faucets,

television, or cars. If you can imagine that, you are on the way to imagining what it was like to live in the Middle Ages. But read on . . .

JULY

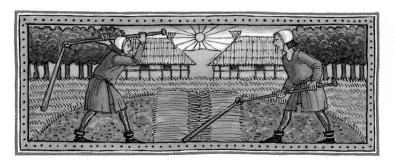

AUGUST

SEPTEMBER

OCTOBER

NOVEMBER

DECEMBER

Cutting parchment to size

Parchmenter shows finished skin to a scribe.

A scribe

An illuminator

Ruling lines on a page

Erasing a script so that the parchment can be reused

Pricking the parchment to mark out the lines

Making a quill pen with a knife

A parchmenter

A stationer

Binding a manuscript

A book cover decorated with gold, ivory, and jewels

A CHILD'S EDUCATION

In a songschool children learned to read and to sing the church services.

Imagine that you are an eight-year-old living in the Middle Ages. You probably wouldn't go to school or know how to read or write. (Most people were peasants and didn't need to read or write.) Everything you would need to know you would learn from watching your father or mother. Boys learned to farm and use tools. Girls learned to weave, sew, and cook. Some children were sent to the nearby monastery or abbey to be trained as either a monk or a nun.

A priest tells children Bible stories.

If you were lucky, you might be sent to a songschool. These were run by the Christian Church, which needed boys to sing in the choir. All church services were conducted in Latin. So, in order to participate, the boys had to learn to read Latin. Some parents sent their children, boys and girls, to songschools to learn to read.

Children learned from watching their parents at work.

If you were the child of a noble family, however, you would be sent to live in the manor, or castle, of another lord at the age of seven. Boys would go as pages to learn good manners and to wait at table. Girls would learn how to do needlework, how to spin, and how to manage a large household.

UNIVERSITIES

The final exam at a university

When you think of an exam, you probably think of a quiet hall full of students writing. In the Middle Ages, the final university exam was more like a football match! For their exam, students had to argue in a public debate. If they argued well, they won their degree. The audience applauded when the student won a point and booed when he did not.

Universities first appeared during the Middle Ages. Students began their course at age fourteen. The subjects they studied were known as the "Seven Liberal Arts." They were: writing, speaking, logic, geometry, arithmetic, astronomy, and music. Afterwards, students might go on to study theology or medicine, for example. By the time they had finished, they would have been studying for about eighteen years!

In northern Europe, professors were in charge of the universities, as they are today. But in Italy, it was the students who were in charge of the professors. Professors could be fired, dismissed, sometimes even beaten up if they were late, refused to answer a difficult question, or simply were just too boring!

Music was one of the "Seven Liberal Arts." In the Middle Ages these arts were depicted as people.

9

WHAT PEOPLE THOUGHT

Studying the Stars

In the Middle Ages, your health, personality, future, even the weather, were all believed to be determined by one thing: the stars.

An astrologer makes predictions. With their knowledge of the movements of the stars and planets, astrologers were able to prophesize about the future.

Every court throughout Europe had a resident astrologer. He had a double role: weatherman and fortuneteller, as you can see from this forecast, in 1498:

"November shall be very rainy and tempestuous with great changing of the air and rain, and wind and perhaps snow . . . sons, children and messangers shall not do well this year, for sicknesses and other misfortunes."

He goes on to predict nosebleeds, headaches, tummy aches, carbuncles, and scabs.

In the Middle Ages the universe was thought to work something like a machine with the earth at the center. Here, two angels turn handles that make the sky revolve around the earth.

A major part of an alchemist's science was to make gold from a mysterious substance called "the philosopher's stone." Above, an alchemist works in his laboratory.

That might seem odd, but even today we read horoscopes in magazines, compiled by "astrologers." They study the influence of stars and planets on human affairs. This subject is called "astrology," and in the Middle Ages it was one of the most important.

Medieval doctors believed that bloodletting helped to rid the body of illness and often used leeches for the procedure.

The Future

A scientist named Roger Bacon wrote this amazingly accurate prediction in the thirteenth century.

"One day man will build machines for navigation . . . wagons that move with incredible speed but do not need animals . . . flying machines . . . machines for descending the depths of the sea . . ."

Scientists in the Middle Ages were eager to find a machine that would run forever without anything to drive it. Above is a design for such a "perpetual motion" machine.

Medicine

Medicine was also influenced by astrology. The best time to treat a patient, for example, was calculated from astrological tables.

The body was believed to contain four "humors," or fluids: blood (hot), phlegm (wet), choler (dry), and melancholy (cold). These affected people's moods: too much blood made you cheerful, whereas too much choler made you angry. If one humor dominated, the result was disease and extreme behavior. Bloodletting was one treatment. It involved attaching leeches to the patient's skin to suck out the excess blood.

Some doctors tried different approaches to medicine and made important discoveries. For instance, in the fourteenth century, during an epidemic of the plague, Italian doctors discovered that the disease spread rapidly when healthy people came in contact with the sick. From then on, they isolated sick patients. This was the first step in controlling infectious diseases.

This illustration is from a Bestiary, a popular book about animals known to the medieval world. Some of the creatures, such as unicorns, centaurs, and griffins, were imaginary.

MAKING A BOOK

Books were so valuable that they sometimes were chained in place so they would not be stolen.

Books were very expensive in the Middle Ages. A Bible, for example, cost the same as an ordinary person's wage for the whole year! Today that's about $13,000. Books were so valuable that they were even chained to stop people from stealing them.

Books were so expensive because there were no printing presses and every book had to be copied by hand. It could take over a year for a monk to copy one book! Also, there was no paper. Instead, sheets of parchment or vellum had to be made from sheep or calfskin. A whole flock of sheep was needed for one illuminated Bible.

Special books were "illuminated" by monks. The word means that they were decorated with patterns or pictures painted in bright colors. They were called "illuminated manuscripts."

Monks made all of their own colored inks. One twelfth-century monk described how he made red ink from copper, salt, honey, and urine. The process took him four weeks! Some red inks were made from crushed insects. Sometimes real gold was even used.

The border of an illuminated manuscript

ARTISTS AND PAINTINGS

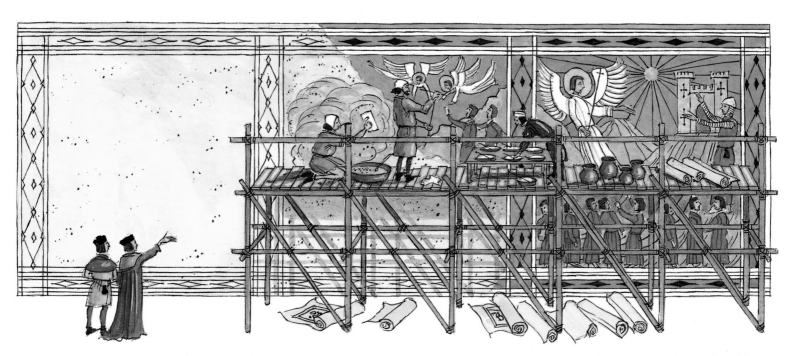

Artists painted frescoes by applying paint directly onto wet plaster. They had to work quickly — before the plaster dried — and could paint only one section at a time.

In the early Middle Ages, artists were not expected to be different or original. Instead, they copied from "pattern books" (which showed objects, animals, people at all angles) or followed precise instructions given by the "patron" who ordered the work. They weren't expected to create realistic paintings either. The most important goal was to tell a story in a painting. Because so many people were illiterate, the only way for them to learn important Bible stories was to look at paintings.

Later, artists tried to show the world as it *really* looked. One revolutionary artist was an Italian named Giotto. For the first time in the history of painting, he tried to show "perspective" (an illusion of depth) in his works.

Most artists worked with "tempera" paint which was made from powdered pigments mixed with egg and water. However, it cracked easily and had to be painted onto special wood. Another method was "fresco" painting, meaning "fresh," because the paint was applied to wet plaster on walls. When the plaster dried, the colors were perfectly preserved, which is why many frescoes you see today are still brightly colored.

An artist paints a picture of the Virgin and Child, a popular subject in the later Middle Ages.

An artist presents an illustrated book to his patron.

RELIGION

The priest celebrates mass.

Pilgrims visit the shrine of a saint.

The abbot

A pilgrim

Giving alms to the poor at the abbey's gate

A knight and his retinue visit the abbey.

LIFE IN AN ABBEY

A scribe works on a manuscript.

Picking herbs to make medicine

A crusader

The master mason

Monks singing in the choir

Tending the sick in the abbey hospital

MONKS AND NUNS

In the Middle Ages going to church was compulsory, at least in Europe — just as going to school is required today. People also had to pay taxes to the Church (the organization), and to follow its laws. The Church was a powerful institution that had enormous influence over people's lives throughout all of Europe. It was headed by the Pope in Rome, who appointed bishops to represent him in every country.

The many different orders of monks and nuns could be identified by their habits. Above are pictured a Benedictine abbot and a Cistercian nun.

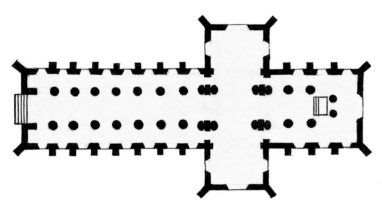

The floor plan for an abbey church shows the typical medieval design. Churches were usually built in the shape of a cross, as a reminder of Christ's death.

Community Life

Many people devoted their entire lives to the Church. You could join a religious community as a monk (if you were a man), or a nun (if you were a woman). Sometimes parents promised their children to these communities as a way of making sure their sons and daughters would never be homeless or without food. If you were talented, it was also a way to become rich and successful.

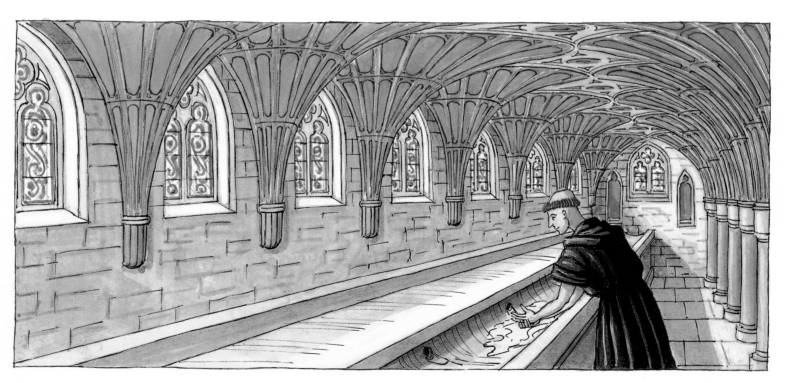

The lavatorium, where monks washed — in cold water

The refectory, where monks ate their meals in silence and listened to readings from the Bible

People in these communities lived together and shared everything they owned. Monks and nuns promised to remain single, to be obedient to their superiors, and to live a life of prayer. They ate simple food, sometimes going without it altogether for several days. This was called "fasting." They wore plain garments, called "habits," and sometimes wore deliberately uncomfortable underclothes, such as hair shirts, which scratched their skin.

Most days were spent in silence, praying or working. There were seven main church services every day, the first one at dawn and the last one in the middle of the night. Monks and nuns didn't often get a good night's sleep.

Hermits

A few people took up the religious life on their own rather than in a community. They were called "hermits," which means recluses. They were thought to be holy and wise. They lived in an isolated, tiny house and often suffered severe physical hardship. Some hermits, especially women, were walled up in their homes with only a hole through which people passed food to them and through which they could give advice on spiritual matters. One early hermit, called St. Simeon the Stylite, sat on top of a pillar for forty-seven years!

A hermit

THE LUXURIOUS HOUSES OF GOD

A church service

Although joining a religious community might not sound like much fun, monks and nuns did not always live as they should and some became very wealthy and powerful.

Wealth and Power

Many communities were wealthy and enjoyed special privileges, often given to them by the king. Some communities owned large pieces of land from which they regularly collected rent. One monastery in Sicily (now part of Italy), for example, was the largest landowner in the country, apart from the king. However, during the Middle Ages many monasteries became centers of learning. They also gave shelter to travelers and aided the poor and the sick.

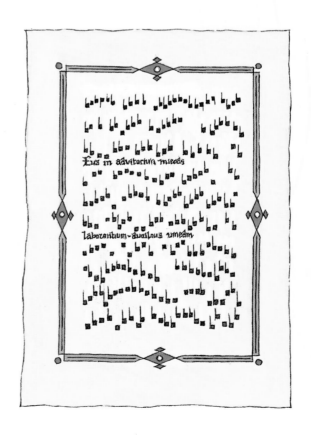

In this page of medieval music the notes are square because of the shape of the quills used to write them.

Visions of Heaven

Imagine how ordinary people must have felt when they went to a cathedral or abbey church for the first time. It was probably the largest, most magnificent building they had ever seen. They gloried in the stained-glass windows, which depicted scenes from the Bible. The church services were conducted in Latin, which very few people could understand. They came, however, to pray and to receive the sacraments. In order to be cleansed of their sins, they went to confession. The priest would make the sign of the cross with his right hand to show them their sins were forgiven. This is still done today.

Well-known incidents in Christ's life were acted out as part of special church services. In monasteries both male and female parts were played by men.

People who were envious of the church's wealth and resented its interference in secular life made fun of the church, as in this drawing of a wolf dressed as a priest.

During a festival, like Easter, there was a special service. A long procession of churchmen wearing dazzling robes would file up the aisle. Choirs chanted sacred music and monks read from large illuminated Bibles and prayer books. Golden cups or crosses, and candlesticks were used, and all this was accompanied by the smell of incense and the flickering light of hundreds of candles. People probably thought they were witnessing a vision of heaven itself.

19

SAINTS AND PILGRIMS

Certain people whose holy lives were observed by those around them came to be venerated as saints and were often prayed to for help after their deaths. Those who traveled to the tombs of saints were known as "pilgrims." Their journeys were known as "pilgrimages."

Saint Francis of Assisi

One of the best-known saints is Saint Francis of Assisi. When he was twenty-one, he gave up a life of wealth to start a religious order based on two ideals: poverty and prayer. His followers were called the "Franciscans." Saint Francis loved nature and called all animals his brothers and sisters.

Saint Francis had a special vision of Christ on the cross. Afterward he found he had wounds in his hands, feet, and side, which were identical to the five wounds that Christ suffered on the cross. These marks are known as the "stigmata." It was a miracle, something out of the ordinary, and people believed it showed that Saint Francis was someone favored by God.

The richly decorated box on top of this shrine contains the remains of a saint. The pedestal underneath had large holes so that pilgrims could get closer to the healing powers of the saint's body.

Saint Francis of Assisi

Relics and Miracles

Many European churches kept the bodies of saints in "shrines," which were like tombs. They thought the remains had special powers that could heal illness, improve harvests, and make other wishes come true. Many pilgrims visited the shrines, hoping for miracles.

Churches also kept parts of the bodies of saints, or objects associated with them, like pieces of clothing. These were called "relics," and they also were thought to have special

A reliquary is a container for relics. This reliquary contains a saint's head.

This scene from a mystery play shows Saint Apollinaire being martyred. All her teeth were pulled out.

powers. They were kept in "reliquaries." One abbey boasted that it owned the coals upon which Saint Lawrence was roasted, Saint Edmund's fingernails, and Saint Thomas's boots! When a saint named Thomas Aquinas died, his fellow monks cut off his head and boiled his body so that they could be sure of keeping his bones as relics.

Not surprisingly, some of the relics were forgeries. For instance, so many people claimed they owned part of Christ's cross that, if all the pieces had actually been put together, many more than just one cross would have been reconstructed!

CRUSADERS AND HERETICS

In the thirteenth century, two twelve-year-old boys led thousands of children from France, Germany, and the Low Countries on a crusade to recover Jerusalem. Unfortunately this crusade ended in failure.

For a Christian, the most important place to visit on a pilgrimage was Jerusalem and the surrounding country, where Christ had lived and died. This was known as the "Holy Land."

In the eleventh century, Jerusalem was taken over by an army of Turks, and Christian pilgrims were no longer allowed to enter the city. In order to try to recover this holy place, European Christian armies launched a series of battle campaigns against the Turks. These were called the "Crusades." The Church encouraged and blessed these "Holy Wars," and the Crusaders thought of themselves as God's warriors.

Many Crusaders, however, went to war just to get rich from raiding and looting the enemy. Many innocent people were wounded or killed. One writer tells of the streets of Jerusalem being piled high with heads, hands, and feet, and inside one of the temples, "men rode in blood up to their knees."

Saladin, the great leader of the Turks, was one of the few real heroes of the Crusades. In one fight against the army of Richard I of England, he saw the king's horse fall. He sent Richard two fresh horses and a groom. As a result of this generous action, Saladin lost the battle.

Crusaders wore the cross of Jerusalem on their tunics to signify the "war of the cross" that they were fighting.

There were many battles during the course of the Crusades which began in 1095 and lasted for nearly 200 years.

The Church was hostile towards non-Christians and even towards other Christians whose beliefs were not exactly the same as those officially taught by the Church. These people were called "heretics." The Church set up a board of inquiry, called the "Inquisition," to find and condemn heretics. The usual punishment for heretics was to be burned to death at the stake.

Many Christian heretics did not actually believe anything outrageous. Some of their beliefs, in fact, were officially adopted by Protestant churches after the Middle Ages. The charge of heresy was often just a convenient way to get rid of the Church's opponents or anyone who was too troublesome.

Others, though, did have extreme ideas. One early group of heretics, for example, called themselves the "Adamites" and wanted to return humankind to its primitive state in the Garden of Eden by practicing nudity. There was also a group called the Albigensians who believed that all matter was evil and that sex itself was sinful. Therefore, their beliefs attacked the very fabric of society.

An inquisitor

Joan of Arc led the French against the English so successfully that the English felt they needed to get rid of her. She was accused of heresy, brought to trial, and burned to death.

LIFE OF THE NOBILITY

A crossbow

A soldier is knighted on the battlefield.

A mounted knight

An archer

A shirt of chain mail

Two knights engage in single combat.

A shield, bearing a coat-of-arms

A warrior bishop with a mace

A squire

A herald

An infantryman with a halberd

An effigy of a knight on a tomb chest

KINGS, LORDS, AND BARONS

The medieval king was really a military leader. He owned a kingdom that needed to be controlled and defended. To help him, he used his rich and powerful subjects, the barons and lords. In return for promising to help him fight his enemies, the king gave the barons and lords areas of land carved out of his kingdom. In theory, the king could reclaim this land whenever he wanted. In practice, the barons became increasingly powerful, and the king did not dare.

This contract between the king and his barons and lords was the basis of a system known as "feudalism." Feudalism was in effect in several European countries during the Middle Ages. It was a political and military system which resulted in everyone in the kingdom having someone ruling over them. The king ruled over the barons, lords, and abbots; the barons ruled over the knights; the abbots ruled over the monasteries; and the lords ruled over the peasants who were given land to farm in exchange for military and other services to the lord.

Seals were made of wax and used to close letters. If the seal was broken, the recipient knew that someone had opened the letter. No royal proclamation was considered genuine if the seal was absent.

At his coronation, the king received his symbols of power: a crown, an orb, and a scepter. This religious ceremony helped to reinforce the belief that the king was appointed by God.

Medieval rulers were always struggling to keep control over ambitious subjects. In order to protect their position, they began to claim that they were God's representatives, not just military leaders. They claimed their power came from God and their right to rule could not be disputed by mere humans.

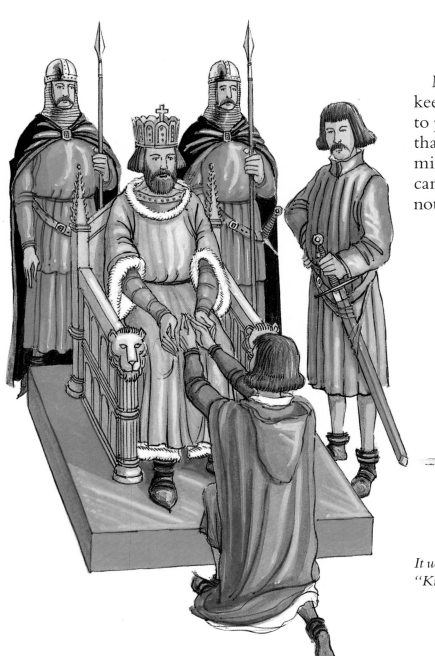

It was believed that sufferers of scrofula, a disease known as the "King's Evil," could by cured by the king's touch.

When a vassal paid homage to his lord, he knelt, placed his clasped hands within those of his lord, and said, "Lord, I become your man."

The barons and lords were known as the king's "vassals." "Vassals" were a bit like servants. They had to fight for the king and help him to control the country. They also had to provide hospitality for the king. (A visit from the king could be very expensive since the royal party might number many hundreds.) They had to attend the king's court when called, keep the king's castles in good order, even look after the kingdom's bridges. There were also other duties — some of them quite bizarre. One king demanded that one of his vassals should "leap, whistle, and break wind" in front of him every Christmas.

This picture of a king receiving his crown from Christ represents the royal claim that a king's rule was God-given and thus could not be disputed by mere mortals.

KNIGHTS AND TOURNAMENTS

If they were to assist the king, the barons needed help themselves, so each baron had his own trained army. The men who fought in the army were called "knights." Whereas the king and his barons spent most of their time ruling the country, the knights spent most of their time learning to fight.

Medieval writers divided society into three classes: those who prayed (monks and nuns), those who labored (peasants, pages), and those who fought (knights). You could not inherit a knighthood or be given it. You had to earn it, and the training took about thirteen years.

When a noble's son was around eight years old, he would go to live in the home of a knight. There he would serve him as a "page" and learn to read, write, wrestle, hawk, ride, sing, and dance. At fourteen, he would go to another knight and serve him as an "esquire." He would learn to use a sword and lance, help his knight at tournaments, and lead his horse to battle. When he was twenty-one, the training was finally completed, and he was ready to become a knight himself.

A knight in training serves as a page.

The ceremony that made an esquire into a knight was called dubbing. First he was bathed to wash away his sins. Then he spent a night alone in prayer. The next day his sword was blessed and given to him, and he took the vows of chivalry (promising to devote himself to good causes). Finally, an older knight struck him on the side of the neck with the flat of the sword, and the ceremony was complete.

Knights fought in tournaments in honor of their ladies. A lady would give a knight her "favor" — a glove or a veil — to wear on his armor as a symbol of her regard.

The famous French knight Jean de Boucicaut could do a somersault, vault onto a horse, and climb up the underside of a ladder using only his hands — all in full armor!

By the late Middle Ages, the most common type of tournaments were "jousts," a series of single combats. They took place inside fenced enclosures called the "lists," and the contestants charged against each other with their lances. The aim was to break the opponent's weapon and unseat him with the lance.

Tournaments also became theatrical entertainments. Knights dressed up as legendary heroes and acted out well-known stories. One knight even appeared as the Goddess Venus with a pair of blond braids!

A knight's armor weighed about sixty-six pounds. That's like carrying a heavy TV around with you! So knights needed to be extremely fit.

Tournaments were an important part of a knight's training. They were mock battles that provided sport and entertainment as well. They gave knights a good opportunity to practice fighting and to show off their skills. Tournaments were dangerous, and many knights were killed in them.

In the siege of the Castle of Love, a mock castle was built, besieged by knights — using flowers, cake, and fruit as missiles — and defended by ladies.

FEASTS

When the lord gave a feast in the great hall of his manor, musicians (called minstrels) provided entertainment. They played their instruments in the minstrels' gallery. The cupbearer, carver, and sewer served the meal. The sewer presented a "subtlety" to his lord. The subtlety was food made often just for show. Here it is a sculpture made from marzipan and covered with gold.

When we celebrate an important occasion, like a birthday or the New Year, we often eat a special meal together. In the Middle Ages, there were many important celebrations, which were called "feast days."

Preparations

Today we like our food to be prepared hygienically. But one medieval cook gave these instructions for making medieval meat jelly: put your hands into the broth to feel it and blow on it regularly!

Because they didn't use forks, food was either mushy, so it could be scooped up on bread, or cut up in small pieces, so it could be picked up with a knife or fingers. The food was always complicated. Guests were offended if anything was served in its natural state because they thought the cooks had not spent enough time preparing it. The ambition of medieval cooks was to create a taste that was entirely new. There are instructions in a French book of household rules, for example, on how to make beef taste like venison (deer meat). It must have been confusing trying to figure out what you were eating.

All of the important guests sat at the high table. An ornament called a nef was placed in front of the most important person at the high table. It was shaped like a boat and sometimes used as a saltcellar or to hold the lord's knife and spoon.

The Feast

A feast usually began at about eleven in the morning and took place in the great hall of the lord's manor or castle. The hall had at one end a table on a platform, called a "dais," where the lord, his family, and the most important guests sat. Along the length of the hall were benches where the rest of the guests were seated.

On the walls, colorful tapestries were hung to decorate the hall and to keep out drafts. Musicians sat in a gallery and played a fanfare as the food was brought in by an army of servants.

Among the most important servants were the "carver," the "cupbearer," and the "sewer." The carver cut up the different meats while the cupbearer carried the cup to anyone who wanted a drink. Only the lord had his own cup—everyone else shared. Sewers served the food and made sure everyone was near a "trencher," a plate made of stale bread from which everyone ate their food. The food was divided into portions called "messes" and shared among several people. Bishops, earls, and viscounts shared with only one other person, and very important people had their own portions.

ENTERTAINMENT

Different classes of nobles hunted with different types of birds. Noblewomen often used merlin hawks (shown here) for hunting. Hunting dogs wore their own special armor. A servant would wave a lure around his head. The lure was a feathered object shaped to resemble the wings of a bird and used to bring the hawk back to the hunter: the hawk thought the lure was its prey, flew toward it, and was recaptured.

Hunting

Hunting was a favorite pastime of the nobility, of kings, barons, lords, and knights. They hunted with dogs and birds of prey, which were highly trained and carefully looked after. King John of England, for example, had his hawks fed on doves, chicken, and pork! Some nobles even visited shrines, hoping to cure a sick bird. Dogs often wore armor as protection against animals like boars and bears. They worked in pairs, catching their prey by the ears and holding it until the hunter came in for the kill. Falcons could kill herons in mid-flight.

Entertainers

Some households had resident entertainers, minstrels or jokers, but others relied on traveling bands of performers who stayed for a night or two and then moved on.

Medieval entertainers had to be good at many things. One thirteenth-century writer specified that a minstrel should be skilled in: storytelling, imitating birdsong, catching little apples on knives, doing card tricks, playing sixteen instruments, and jumping through four hoops!

The aristocracy of medieval Europe loved to hear about the adventures of knights carrying out heroic deeds and falling in love with beautiful ladies. The most famous stories were about the Emperor Charlemagne and his knights, and about King Arthur and the Knights of the Round Table.

The knights of the stories were always brave. They fought dragons and giants to rescue princesses or to win their lady's favor. The ladies were demanding and disdainful. This sacrificial love of the knights for their ladies became known as "Courtly Love."

This was sometimes a painful experience for the knights. One heroine ordered the knight Aurelius to prove himself by picking up all the stones on the beaches of Brittany in France. When he heard what he had to do, Aurelius felt so hopeless that he went to bed for two years.

The court jester was often the companion and confidant of the lord himself. The jester held a stick, with something that looks like a balloon attached to it, that made funny noises.

The game of chess was invented by the Chinese and introduced into Europe in the ninth century by the Arabs. At first, Europeans played the game using real people instead of pieces!

LIFE IN THE COUNTRY

Ploughing

A blacksmith's forge

A steward

A bailiff

Treading grapes

Thatching houses

A MEDIEVAL MANOR AND ITS ESTATES

Women spinning and carding

Salting meat

A woodcutter

A poacher

A peasant's fireside

The Great Hall of the manor

THE LORD AND HIS MANOR

Ordinary peasants lived on land lent to them by the local lord. Lords (people like barons, knights, and abbots) were given the land by the king. The lord lived in a large manor house or castle and lent out his lands to the peasants. In return for living on the land, the peasants promised the lord to work on his land and to give him various things. They were called his "villeins" (a sort of servant).

Millers provided the village with flour. Power for the mill that ground the grain came from the windmill.

Since honey was the main sweetener for food and drink, bees were valuable in the Middle Ages. Sugar, introduced into Europe in the twelfth century, was rare and expensive. Beeswax was used to make candles, although they were very expensive. One candle could cost as much as a whole day's wages.

This system is called the "feudal system," which was common throughout Europe.

Peasants rarely needed to buy or sell anything. They grew or made everything they needed themselves. All of them worked as farmers, and some had another job as well. One man was the village blacksmith, who made all the metal things for the villagers, for example. Women spun sheep's wool to make cloth for clothes.

Some villages in Europe were required to pay dues to the lord by giving him eggs at Easter. Another due was the fee paid if a girl from one village married a boy from another.

The villagers were roughly divided into two groups: "freemen" and "serfs." "Freemen" were peasants who had saved up enough money to pay rent for their land. They didn't have to work for the lord and could move away from the manor.

"Serfs," however, "belonged" to the lord. The only way they could leave the manor was by buying their freedom (as freemen did), joining holy orders, or marrying a free woman. Many were probably content to remain serfs, especially if they had a sympathetic lord.

The hayward was a manor official employed to ensure that animals did not stray onto arable land (land used for planting).

Most peasants lived in villages. The typical village would have a manor house, where the lord lived, a church, and twenty to thirty huts for the peasants.

Peasants built their own huts. They were made from a timber frame and filled with "wattle and daub," a mixture of mud, straw, and animal hair. Their roofs were thatched or tiled, and they normally had two rooms: one for the family and one for animals. The roof space was used for storing hay. The earth floor was covered with straw, and there were holes in the walls for windows. There was no glass because it was too expensive. Inside, the rooms would have been dark and smoky from the hearth fire in the center.

The beadle collected fines for the lord. The lord, who was in charge of the law in his villages, made a lot of money from these fines because he could keep them for himself.

PEASANTS AT WORK

January: Feasting continued from December 25 to January 6, the Feast of Epiphany.

April: As the crops began to grow, there was a feeling of anticipation of the year ahead.

February: No work was done in the fields, and peasants stayed indoors to keep warm.

May: With warm weather, outdoor life began again. May was dedicated to the noble sport of hunting.

March: In wine-producing areas grape vines were prepared in early spring.

June: The feast of Barnabas in June was the traditional time to start the haymaking.

Most manors had three large fields. One was for growing wheat, another for barley, and the third rested or "lay fallow." Each field was divided into long, narrow strips with thin grassy paths between them. The strips of land were hardly ever next to one another so peasants with neighboring strips often agreed to pool their land and farm it together, sharing their tools. Outside these fields was common land, where animals could graze. Down by the river was the meadowland, where the long grass was cut, dried, and stored as hay for the winter.

The villages were often isolated. Roads were very bad, hardly more than tracks, and for long periods of the winter the village was probably cut off from other villages. The great main roads built by the Romans were still used, and a network of minor roads had been added since. They were difficult to maintain, especially as people used to dig in them for clay to mend their homes. As a result, great holes

July: The heavy work of the summer months continued with the corn harvest.

October: The harvest completed, it was time to sow seeds for next year's crops.

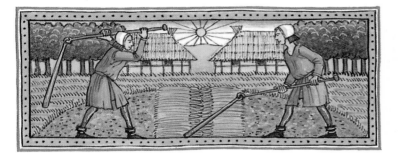

August: The grain was threshed — the seeds were separated from the stalks.

November: In preparation for winter, wood was gathered to use as fuel.

September: With the coming of autumn, it was time to harvest and press the grapes for making wine.

December: Since there was not enough food for the long winter months, animals were slaughtered for eating.

were left in the roads, which made journeys even more dangerous. One miller, for example, in the fifteenth century dug a large, deep hole in the middle of the road. It filled with rainwater, and a traveling glovemaker fell into it and drowned along with his horse.

The Calendar

If you asked a medieval peasant what the date was, he would probably only have been able to tell you whether it was winter or summer. Precise dates didn't matter to peasants. Their lives were dominated by the natural rhythms of the seasons. Their calendar for the year was a succession of agricultural activities — plowing, sowing, harvesting. The exact date was irrelevant. In medieval calendars, the particular jobs for each month were illustrated. These are known as the "Labors of the Months" and can be found in sculptures, woodcarvings, and illuminated manuscripts.

PEASANTS AT HOME

The inside of a peasant's home was very dark and smoky. For light, peasants used tallow candles made from animal fat, which gave off a strong smell.

The center of a peasant's home was the fire. This provided all of the heat and most of the light. Water was boiled over the fire, food cooked in it, and meat smoked in the chimney. (Meat went bad quickly because there was no way to keep it cold. Smoking was one way to preserve it.)

Peasants had only two meals a day. In the morning they might have eaten dark bread and cheese. In England, they drank ale (a bit like beer) — even the children drank it. No one chose to drink water if there was something else. In the evening, after a hard day's work, they ate from the "cauldron." This was a large pot with a stew of oatmeal, beans, or rabbit, for example.

At the back of the peasant's house was a small area of land called a "croft." Plants and strong-tasting vegetables and herbs such as leeks, onions, garlic, and sage were grown in it. Their flavor added interest to the food and also helped to disguise the taste of bad meat. The croft might also contain a few fruit trees or vines from which drinks like cider or wine could be made. In winter, fuel was also stored in the croft.

A peasant shears his sheep. Sheep were more valuable for their coats than for their meat. A serf was not allowed to sell wool without his lord's permission.

Most of the peasant's animals were killed in the late autumn. Their meat was salted or smoked to preserve it. The animals that were kept alive during winter were kept in the croft.

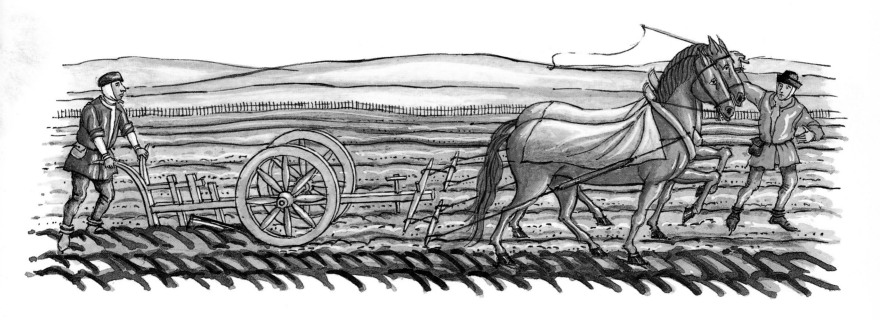

When the heavier plow was introduced, horses had to be used because oxen were too slow. The invention of the horseshoe in the early Middle Ages made it easier on the horse's feet, and the development of a new type of harness took the strain off its neck.

Parish priests were often of peasant stock and were not always literate. The land the priest farmed was called a "glebe."

Peasants' lives became easier toward the end of the Middle Ages. By the eleventh century, farming techniques had improved and harvests were better. A heavier plow was developed, for example, which could turn over wet, clayey soils. With the help of this plow, more land could be used for farming.

When a harvest was poor and stocks of food failed to last through the winter, families sometimes starved to death. Many were tempted to "poach" (steal animals) from their lord's land. But the punishments for poaching were very harsh. Killing a deer, for example, was punishable by death.

Peasants did have some time for other things besides work. They enjoyed many "holy days" (which is where the word "holidays" comes from). At Christmas, the peasants went to special church services. Afterward, there were sports, dancing, and plenty of ale. On feast days, such as Christmas, everyone went to the lord's manor for a grand meal and, often, entertainment.

Robin Hood was a famous outlaw who became an English folk hero. His poaching activities and robbing the rich to help the poor made him a champion of the people.

LIFE IN THE TOWNS

A watchman at the city gates

A borough charter

A rich burgher

A pedlar

A butcher slaughters an animal in the gutter.

A water fountain

A beggar receives alms.

A lady in a litter

A moneylender

The Lord Mayor

Rotten meat is burned under the nose of the offending butcher.

The coat of arms of a guild

BUYING AND SELLING

Most people lived and worked on the land during the Middle Ages. Farming methods were inefficient, so most of the population was needed to farm the land for food. It was only when farming methods improved, from the eleventh century onward, that some people could move away from farming and find other ways to make a living. This is how the first towns developed.

Merchants and craftsmen were the two main groups of people who came together to create towns. Merchants bought goods in one place and sold them elsewhere at a profit. Craftsmen made the goods and sold them at enough profit to make a living.

These early towns were relatively independent of the lords who owned the land on which they were built. The townspeople paid the lord rent in return for their freedom. They were able to trade freely, run their own courts, and work independently. The towns were often fortified, that is, protected by high walls, and had their own small army in case the lord tried to go back on his agreement. The

Women were usually responsible for brewing and were called brewsters. When the ale was ready, they stuck a small bush into their front wall to attract customers.

towns had their own government, led by a lord mayor. His announcements, along with any other important news, were made public by a town crier with a bell. To reduce crime, no one was allowed outside after a certain time in the evening. The narrow, unlit streets were an excellent place for robbers and thieves to hide.

Merchants often needed to borrow money. Many moneylenders dealt only in small amounts, but there were some powerful banking families, mostly Italian, who lent money on a grand scale. The Medici family was one of the most famous.

Every trade had a different sign to identify it: fish for fishmongers, scissors for drapers, a boot for cobblers, and a bush for taverns. Since most people could not read, these signs were essential.

Houses in towns were usually made from a wooden framework filled with "wattle and daub." If the townspeople needed another room, they just built another floor on top of the first. The upper rooms often jutted forward over the street, so that they were very close to the houses opposite. Fire was, therefore, a constant hazard.

In many towns water was piped in to public fountains from outside the town walls. This source was not always sufficient and was often supplemented by streams and wells, which were easily infected. Water carriers provided a more reliable alternative, but their services were not free.

Jugglers performed at fairs, which were held at various times of the year.

Streets were narrow, winding, cobbled, and very dirty. Parts of the town opened into more spacious areas, like the market square and the public fountain. Most houses had enough space at the back to keep a few animals, and some people farmed small areas of land outside the town walls. Some of the bigger houses had courtyards and pleasure gardens.

There were no shops as we know them. Craftsmen worked on the ground floor of a house in a long, narrow room opening onto the street. They displayed what they had made at the front of their workshops.

THE GUILDS

At the end of their apprenticeships, young trainees had to produce a masterpiece — a piece of work for inspection. If the masterpiece was accepted, they were allowed to become masters of their trade.

The bakers' guild paid for this stained glass window. They are pictured at the bottom of it, carrying bread.

Each group of craftsmen had its own "guild," which was somewhat like a club. A craftsman was not allowed to practice his trade unless he belonged to it. The guild protected the group from outside competition and kept standards high.

Secrets of the trade were passed on by the master to his apprentice, or trainee. The apprentices were not allowed to share these secrets with anyone outside the guild. Each guild had its own set of rules. An apprentice, for example, had to serve a master for seven years before he could set up shop on his own. To discourage shoddy workmanship, one French guild instructed its tailors to spend a day mending clothes for the poor whenever they spoiled a piece of cloth.

Craftsmens' workshops were often clustered together in one area of a town. Some street names, dating from medieval times, give us a clue as to which trades were practiced in which areas: "Ironmonger Lane," "Corn Market," "Masons' Yard," "Leather Lane," "Threadneedle Street."

The names of some guilds give us other clues as well. The "Barber-Surgeons' Guild," for example, tells us that barbers were once qualified to cut off more than just people's hair.

Despite guild regulations, some members were guilty of such dishonest practices as watering the wine.

46

ENTERTAINMENT

Mystery plays were performed on special feast days and showed scenes from the Bible.

One of the grandest entertainments were the "mystery plays," which took place on special feast days. They were performed either on a fixed stage in the market square or on the back of a wagon. Each guild acted out a particular scene from the Bible. One of the favorite scenes was Noah's ark. There were also villains like Lucifer and Herod, at whom the audience could hiss and boo.

Traveling players, acrobats, and musicians entertained people on more ordinary days. Sports like football, wrestling, and a rougher version of blindman's buff were popular.

Sometimes players were even killed. In winter, people skated on frozen rivers and ponds (they made their skates from animal bones).

In the early Middle Ages, tales were told by professional storytellers to a listening audience. Later, as people learned to read and more books became available, more people were able to read by themselves.

The ideal of medieval town life was to find a good balance between work and play. As one writer put it, "a city should not only be commodious (convenient) and serious, but also merry and sportful."

A professional storyteller

People made their ice skates from animal bones and pushed themselves along the ice with sticks.

FAMILY LIFE

People died when they were quite young in the Middle Ages. Most lived only about thirty years. There were many incurable diseases. It was common for girls, and sometimes boys, to marry in their mid-teens. (It was a disgrace if you weren't married by twenty!) Parents arranged the marriages without even asking their children. The wife was then expected to have as many children as possible (often about eight) since only half might live to be adults. The wife herself might even die while having a baby.

This comic picture of a wife beating her husband does not represent common medieval practice. Customarily the husband ruled the household, and his wife was legally his property.

Medieval households were very crowded, much more so than is common today. Families lived all together. Parents, children, grandparents, and unmarried aunts and uncles often lived in one house. Even people who were not relatives, such as servants and apprentices, would live there too. Except for the very wealthy, who owned large houses, there was little privacy at home. At night, everyone slept in the same room.

Parents with their children

Beds were the most valued piece of furniture in the house. Curtains were meant primarily to keep out drafts.

Children were not shown much obvious affection. The general attitude seemed to be that the sooner they grew up the better.

48

WHAT PEOPLE WORE

Medieval women wore horned headdresses and men wore liripipes — hoods with a long point that sometimes reached the ground. It became fashionable for men to wind these hoods around their heads like a turban. Toward the end of the Middle Ages, men's shoes became more and more pointed. Sometimes the points were so long they had to be tied to the ankle. Knights at the battle of Nicopolis cut off these long toes so they would not trip as they retreated from the battlefield. Children were dressed as miniature adults. The church tried to curb extravagant fashions by passing "sumptuary laws," which limited the amount of expensive material or the number of bright colors that could be used.

Wool and linen were the most common materials used for clothing. Peasant men wore coarse tunics, leggings, and wooden clogs or shoes of thick cloth. Peasant women wore long dresses of rough cloth and hoods on their heads.

For the clothes of the wealthy, however, silk (from Italy), velvet, and a heavy cloth called "damask" (from Damascus) were often used. Fur, such as squirrel or ermine, was used for linings and trimmings. Children were dressed like miniature adults.

In the later Middle Ages, a taste for luxury clothing developed among the wealthy. Clothes became a symbol of how rich and important you were.

Women wore clothes that were difficult to move about in. They were meant to show that the wearer was a lady of leisure; she didn't need to move around quickly like working women. But her clothes were sometimes so impractical that she had to be carried about in a portable chair, called a "litter."

Rich people were so concerned that peasants should not look like them that they even made it a crime for peasants to wear nice clothes. A law said that:

"No plowman, oxherd, cowherd, shepherd, swineherd, dairywoman, or anyone else who works as a farmer should wear anything but cheap cloth or blanket."

HEALTH AND HEALING

Doctors at the University of Bologna in Italy were among the first to dissect human corpses.

Eyeglasses, an Arab invention, were imported into Europe in the late Middle Ages.

Towns were unhealthy places to live in and disease spread quickly through the crowded streets and houses. In the center of the streets was a kind of gutter into which everyone threw their rubbish, dead dogs, and sewage.

In the home, things weren't much better. There were no flushing toilets and usually a chamberpot was used. It was emptied out of an upstairs window into the gutter below. Unfortunately, the contents often landed on passersby. It was very unusual for people to take baths. Writers of the time thought it worth noting that King John of England took a bath as often as once every three weeks.

There were few doctors and they charged a lot of money for treating people. Even so, they didn't know how to cure many diseases. There were some very strange practices. A surgeon might treat a deranged patient by cutting open his skull to let the devil out. Or someone with a sore throat might try to cure it by hanging a magpie's beak around his neck. Yet, at the same time, important advances were being made. At Bologna University doctors first began to dissect corpses to find out how the human body worked.

Many people believed that the plague was a judgment from God. During epidemics, religious processions were organized and plague crosses held up as a sign of penance or as an apology to God. Flagellants whipped themselves as a punishment for their sins.

The "Black Death"

Fatal epidemics were frequent in medieval Europe. But the terrible plague called the "Black Death" that hit Europe was worse than all the others because of the speed with which it spread, its deadliness, and the number of people it affected. In just one year, from 1348 to 1349, almost half of the population of Europe died. Whole villages were wiped out, and there were not enough people left alive to bury the dead.

One writer described the plague like this: "It first showed itself as lumps under the arms or between the legs. Some of these grew as large as apples . . . The lumps soon spread all over the body. Black or purple spots then appeared . . . These spots were a sure sign of death."

Lepers were sometimes isolated in special hospitals outside the town walls. Isolation reduced the spread of the disease, which was almost eradicated in Europe by the end of the Middle Ages.

THE WIDER WORLD

A galley ship rowed by oarsmen

Chinese porcelain

A merchant

A sailor

Perfumes and spices

A merchant from Asia shows silks to a tradesman.

SHIPS IN PORT

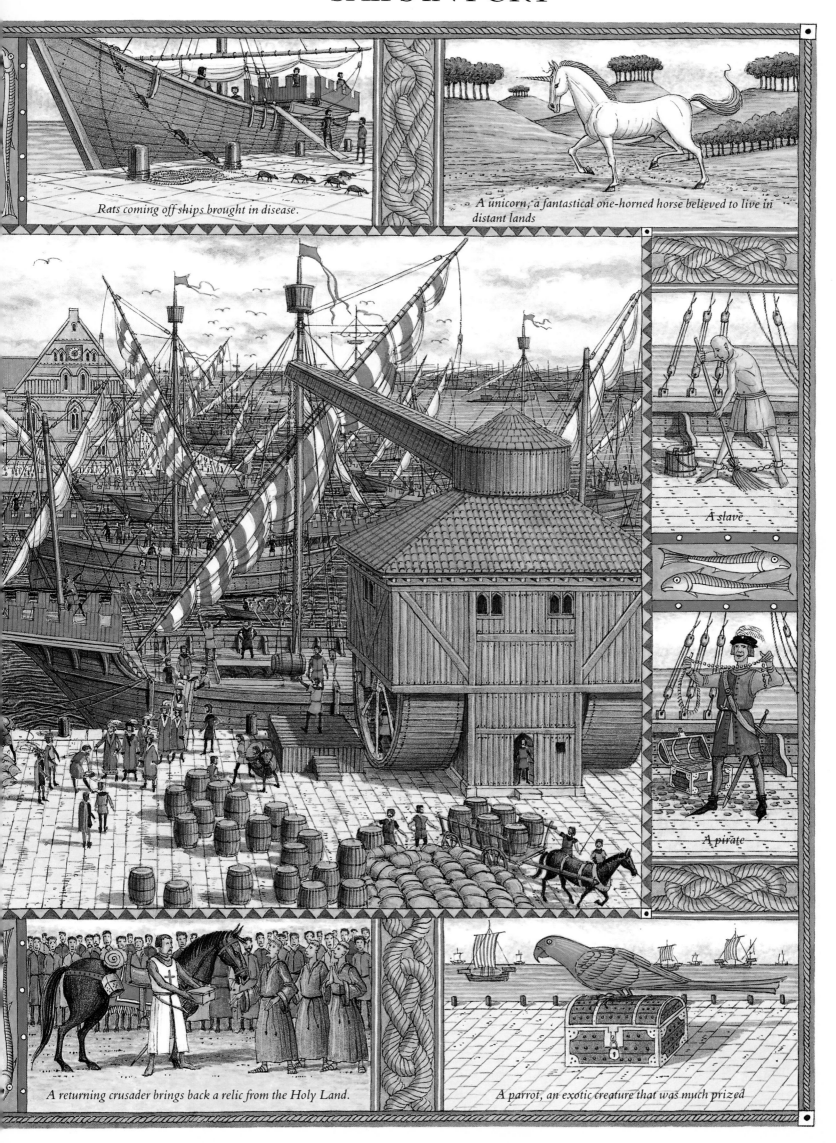

Rats coming off ships brought in disease.

A unicorn, a fantastical one-horned horse believed to live in distant lands

A slave

A pirate

A returning crusader brings back a relic from the Holy Land.

A parrot, an exotic creature that was much prized

NAVIGATORS AND EXPLORERS

Marco Polo, the great medieval explorer, traveled in the East for seventeen years and wrote about his travels.

Today we can travel quickly and easily from one country to another. With television and newspapers, we also know almost immediately what is happening on the other side of the world. In the Middle Ages, things were very different.

Most people didn't travel much. There were few good roads, and it could take a day to travel just twenty-five miles which takes less than an hour by car today. Very few people ever left their own country. Without any planes, journeys had to be made by sea which was slow, uncomfortable, and often dangerous.

Little was known about distant lands, and no one in Europe knew that America or Australia even existed. It was left to the scholars to theorize about distant lands and what went on there. Many believed, for example, that the earth was flat with a great ocean around its edges. Early travelers were afraid they might fall off the edge if they traveled too far. Some pilgrims and early traders returned with fantastic tales of strange creatures living in distant lands: unicorns, men with faces in their chests, and one-legged people who used their one huge foot as a sunshade.

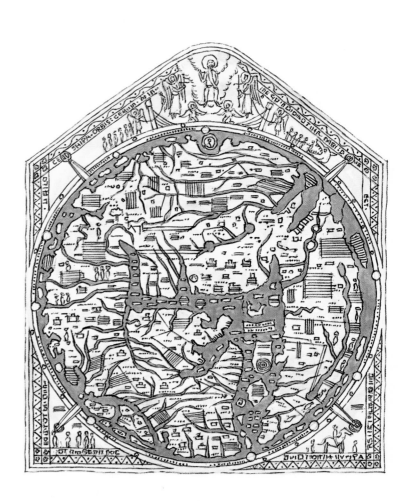

This map of the world shows the three continents known to the medieval world: Africa, Asia, and Europe. Because Jerusalem was so important to Christians, it is shown as being at the center of the world.

Beginning in the thirteenth century, sailors who carried the merchants by sea began to chart, or make maps of, the coastlines of the lands they had "discovered" and the routes they had taken. Such recordkeeping was made possible as a result of three important discoveries passed on from the Arabs. These were the compass, the astrolabe, and the quadrant. These navigational instruments enabled sailors to tell the exact time, distance, and direction of their journeys.

A sciapod was an imaginary creature believed to lie on its back and shade itself from the sun with its foot.

This picture of the Adoration of the Magi shows one king as an African, one as an Asian, and one as a European, representatives from each of the known continents.

Although initially no one traveled to explore these lands, the growth of towns changed all this.

Many of the richer townspeople earned a living by buying and selling. Ambitious merchants wanted to discover new markets in which to sell. They also wanted to find new types of goods to sell. And so they traveled.

Some explorers wrote down what they saw and gave advice to travelers who might follow them. Marco Polo, an Italian living at the end of the thirteenth century, made his way overland from Venice to China. This route became known as the "Silk Route."

An astrolabe (above left) was an instrument used to measure the movement of the stars.

The compass (above right) was a Chinese invention introduced into Europe in the twelfth century. With the help of a compass, sailors could explore unknown seas without losing their way.

TRADING WITH DISTANT LANDS

When you go to a store, you probably see lemons, melons, apricots, or rice. Do you put sugar or pepper on your food? Do you have a mirror in your house? If you had lived in the early Middle Ages, you would probably never have seen any of these things. By the end of the Middle Ages, most of them were well known in Europe. What had happened?

This map shows where such spices as pepper, cinnamon, nutmeg, and mace came from.

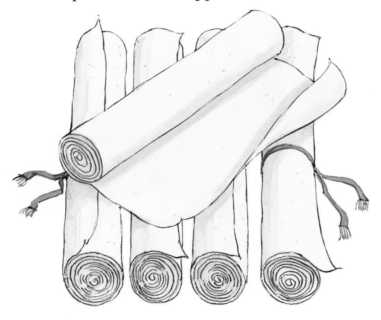

Paper was invented in China in the first century A.D. *but was rarely used in Europe before the end of the Middle Ages, despite the fact that it was much cheaper than parchment or vellum.*

The answer is that people had begun to travel abroad and had brought these things back with them.

Crusaders, returning from battles in the Holy Land, brought back exotic goods, such as lemons, melons, apricots, rice, cottons, perfumes, rugs, and mirrors. They also brought back new ideas.

The Italian cities of Genoa and Venice were bitter trade rivals. The picture shows a fight at sea between Genoan and Venetian merchant ships.

Russian merchants carry furs, which were the main Russian export.

Near the end of the Middle Ages, traders became interested in precious metals and gems, such as diamonds and gold, which were found in Africa. A Portuguese prince, Henry (later called "Henry the Navigator"), gathered together a group of shipbuilders, astronomers, cartographers (mapmakers), and sailors, and set off to explore the west coast of Africa. His sailors were frightened at first, fearing that the tropical sea might boil them up. In 1441, his expedition returned with two cargoes: a parcel of gold and a group of African captives. Trade in human beings had begun and would later develop into the notorious slave trade.

Survivors of a shipwreck off the coast of England had little hope of being rescued, because English law stated that the cargo from wrecks was the property of the finders — unless there were survivors!

From the East, merchants brought luxury goods like carpets and precious cloth such as Chinese silk. As much as possible, they followed routes already pioneered by others. One of these was the "Silk Route." The most important and most valuable trade with the East, however, was in spices. These are seasonings like pepper, cinnamon, nutmeg, and mace. They were very rare and much sought after in the Middle Ages.

NEW DISCOVERIES AND INVENTIONS

The first printing press

When Christian crusaders returned from wars in the Holy Land, not only did they bring back new goods, but they also brought back new ideas. They had learned much from their enemies, the Muslims, while living in the Holy Land.

In the early twelfth century, people in Europe wrote the numbers 1 to 10 like this: I II III IV V VI VII VIII IX X. For 100, they wrote C, and for 1,000, they wrote M. These numbers had been learned from the Romans and are called Roman numerals. They are still used sometimes, on watch faces for example. But it is difficult to add and subtract with them because Romans didn't use a zero in their numbers.

One group of Muslims, called Arabs, had worked out new numbers. They are Arabic numerals, and they are the ones we use today. It was much easier to add and subtract with them. They were brought back to Europe by the Christian crusaders.

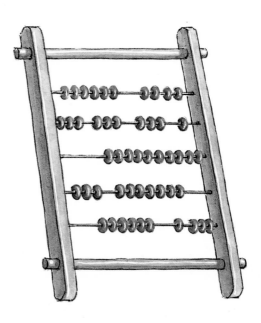

The abacus, a machine for counting, was probably invented in China.

Arab mathematicians also had produced a series of mathematical tables to help them figure out the size of things. These trigonometry tables were brought back to Europe, and are still used today to calculate the sizes of angles.

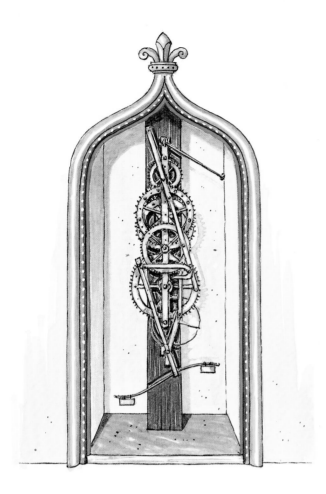

The mechanical clock was introduced into Europe in the thirteenth century. Before the mechanical clock, people used water clocks and sundials or guessed the time from the position of the sun.

Gunpowder eventually revolutionized warfare, but it took some time for Europeans to get used to it. The giant guns were probably as dangerous to the soldiers firing them as they were to the enemy. In 1460, during a siege in Scotland, the Scottish king, some of his nobles, and the gun crew were all killed by an exploding cannon barrel. Hand guns were no more successful when they were first introduced. At the Battle of Towton, in 1461, the soldiers armed with guns could manage only one shot an hour.

Buttons were introduced from the East in the fourteenth century.

A New Weapon

The Chinese first invented gunpowder, which was used mostly for firework displays. When gunpowder was introduced into Europe in the fourteenth century, it was used for war.

Paper money was a Chinese invention.

A New Way to Make Books

A more peaceful invention was printing. The Chinese had invented it before gunpowder, but it did not reach Europe until the late fourteenth century.

Printed books could be produced quickly, cheaply, and more accurately. Also, more people could afford to buy their own books which gave a great boost to the spread of knowledge. It also signaled the dawn of a new age of learning called the Renaissance.

PIECING THE CLUES TOGETHER

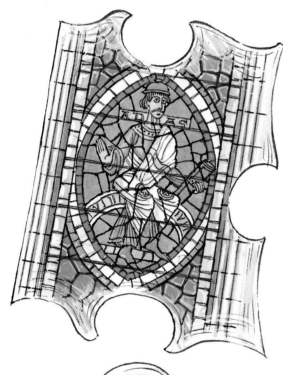

There are many unsolved mysteries and unanswered questions about the Middle Ages. However, we have learned much from historians, who have picked up clues from various pieces of "evidence." This "evidence" might be found in medieval books, buildings, or paintings. Historians are really a bit like detectives. They pick up clues and try to piece together the full story. We can all be historians. Here are some sources of evidence you can try exploring for yourself.

If you have been to a city, town, or village in Europe, you probably saw at least one medieval building, or part of one. Medieval churches are the most common. Inside the church there are probably stained-glass windows, carvings, or wall paintings. There are also medieval walls, stone arches, or the stone frames of old windows built into the fabric of more modern buildings. (You can find out where buildings like these are located from your local library, tourist office, or museum.)

By looking at these buildings in person or in books, you can pick up many clues about

medieval life. Try to imagine how the buildings once looked. If you want to know how a building was built, a ruin will be more useful to you. Take note of where the building stands. Its location can give you important clues about its original use. A remote site next to an old medieval road might once have been a wayside chapel. A site next to a narrow stretch of fast-flowing water might have been a water mill. A ruin on a hilltop might once have been a fort.

Visiting a museum or art gallery is a good way to pick up clues. Medieval art tells us a lot about the Middle Ages. Look at the costumes of the people in a painting, for example. A painting of the Nativity might show the Three Kings dressed in medieval costume, or a painting of The Last Supper might show a table full of medieval food.

Piecing together different clues is rather like doing a jigsaw puzzle. As the different pieces fit together, you can watch the jigsaw begin to take shape and the world of the Middle Ages come to life.

TIME CHART

Date	LEARNING AND THE ARTS	EXPLORATION AND DISCOVERY
300 – 400		
400 – 500		
500 – 600		
700 – 800		
800 – 900		Game of *chess* introduced into Europe from China
1000 – 1100	1030 The Medical School established in Salerno, Italy 1088 The School of Law established in Bologna, Italy	*Paper* introduced into Europe from China
1100 – 1200	1135 – 83 *Chrétien de Troyes*, French poet who wrote many romantic stories about King Arthur and his Knights of the Round Table 1140 *Saint-Denis*, the first Gothic cathedral, built 1154 The University of Paris, the *Sorbonne*, founded 1170 The *University of Oxford* founded in England	Navigational instruments — the ship's *compass*, *astrolabe*, and *quadrant* — introduced into Europe *Sugar* introduced into Europe
1200 – 1300	1229 The *University of Cambridge* founded in England 1214 – 92 *Roger Bacon*, English scientist 1225 – 74 *St. Thomas Aquinas*, who wrote about Christian doctrine 1266 – 1337 *Giotto*, Italian artist	1254 – 1324 *Marco Polo*, Italian explorer First *mechanical clocks* used in Europe
1300 – 1400	1340 – 1400 *Geoffrey Chaucer*, English poet of the Canterbury Tales 1335 – 1405 *Jean Froissart*, who wrote about the history of France	*Gunpowder* introduced into Europe from China; used on the battlefield to fire cannonballs
1400 – 1500		First *handguns* used in Europe 1394 – 1460 *Henry the Navigator* 1454 *Printing* from movable type invented by *Johann Gutenberg* in Germany

THE CHURCH	NOBLES AND PEASANTS
313 The *Edict of Milan*, issued by the Roman Emperor, Constantine, making Christianity legal in the Roman Empire	
480 – 550 *St. Benedict*, founder of the Benedictine monastic order	
	Arthur, legendary leader of the Romano-British against the Saxon invaders, later made into the hero of many stories
	800 *Charlemagne*, king of the Franks, the most powerful tribe in Western Europe, crowned Holy Roman Emperor
1084 *St. Bruno*, founder of the Carthusian order	**1043 – 99** *"El Cid,"* Spanish hero
1095 The *First Crusade* called at the Council of Clermont	**1066** *The Battle of Hastings:* Normans, led by William the Conqueror, defeat British and invade England
	1086 *The Domesday Survey*, recording the everyday life of England, completed
1144 The *Second Crusade*	
1187 The *Third Crusade*	
1203 The *Fourth Crusade*	**1215** *The Magna Carta* (the "Great Charter"): signed by King John to limit certain powers of the monarchy
1212 The *Children's Crusade*	
1217 The *Fifth Crusade*	
1181 – 1226 *St. Francis of Assisi*, founder of the Franciscan order	
1216 – 1221 *St. Dominic*, founder of the Dominican order	
1232 *The Inquisition*, to root out "heresy," set up by Frederick II, Holy Roman Emperor	
1290 The Jews expelled from England (allowed to return in 1656)	
	1366 – 1421 *Jean Boucicaut*
	1337 – 1453 *Hundred Years' War* between England and France
	1348 – 51 *The Black Death*
	1358 *The Jacquerie Revolt*: French peasant rebellion in reaction to imposition of new taxes (revolt violently crushed)
	1381 *The Peasants' Revolt* in England (revolt crushed)
1479 *The Spanish Inquisition* set up to deal with Jewish and Muslim "heretics"	**1412 – 31** *St. Joan of Arc*
1492 The Jews expelled from Spanish territory	**1453** Constantinople (modern-day Istanbul), capital of the Christian Byzantine Empire in Eastern Europe throughout the Middle Ages, taken by the Turks
1492 *Christopher Columbus* discovered America	**1492** Granada, the last Muslim stronghold in Spain, taken by Ferdinand of Castile, who then became the first Christian king of a united Spain

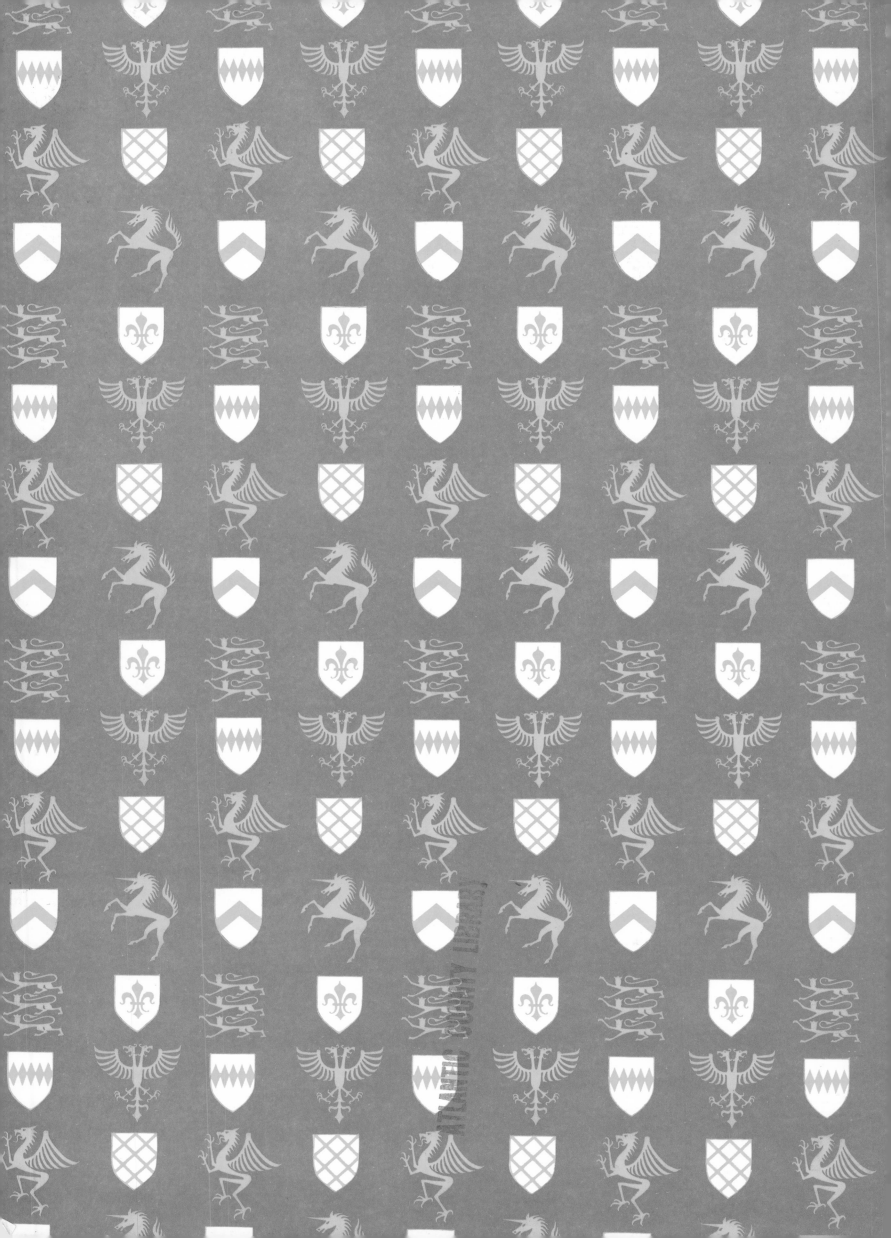